# oh orchid o'clock

"Though I than He – may longer live/He longer must – than I –": so Emily Dickinson marked how poetry, and guns, break temporality. Endi Bogue Hartigan, in this wondrous and fearsome mélange of meditation, rhyme, and wordwelding, pursues the vortex of Dickinson's dark conjuncture even as she mounts a Blakean charge against the modern tyranny of clock-time. Her *oh orchid o'clock* is rife with natural and mechanical marvels—scent clocks and snowflakes, marigolds and gym ellipticals—but its terribly ubiquitous mechanisms are the Taylorized workplace and the AR-15. Counter to these rapacious devices, Hartigan weaves a lush tangle of perceptions, drawn from the everyday, heightened by her deliriously acute ear. Not a knife-beak, not an ink fluke: public events toll ever more ominously in her Northwestern US, and yet these poems, lounging in the clock like certain creatures, lyrically undo the incremental fiction of the hours.

—John Beer, author of *Lucinda*

Endi Bogue Hartigan's *oh orchid o'clock* fluidly rotates constructions of time: our violent times ("America's deadliness" and "unimaginable shootings"); scientific and philosophical time ("the topography of time-space"); the "orbit" of digital time we frequently "visit"; the transportive materiality of deep time ("the cuckoo in the dark wormhole of the clock"); the ruling "grip of time" within the timepiece; the illusory "streaming of time" that is "a perception trick"; and, critically, time "resolved" or defeated by nature, by "the orchid opal sky calculating nothing," by the imprecision of water, which is "the nemesis of all clocks," by fire, where the "clock surrounds… a foliage of flame, clockless." Here, in the book's free rotation of poetic time, which is "something pure and round," we are not "absorbed" by the "vertical worlds" that "fall horizontally." Here, in the linguistic rotations constructed by poetry, we are not mere visitors of time or "…tethered as a clockhand." Here, in *oh orchid o'clock*, we are new rotations, where "one side of the orchid is pointing at everything close."

—Amy Catanzano, author of *Starlight in Two Million: A Neo-Scientific Novella*

Open *oh orchid o'clock*, and you find yourself inside the clockwork maze of a Chinese incense box that releases each hour with a distinct scent. Let the hours teach, sing, dismantle and restore. These poems by Endi Bogue Hartigan fathom time's mythos in nesting dolls and gunshots, measures in galactic orbits and fractals or intervals between ravages and respite as by the Nilometer—the unit that ancient Egyptians used to calculate the precisely rising levels of the Nile between successive flooding. Hartigan's work shows us the cuckoo in the clock but also the clock in the cuckoo: how time resides in the body, grips the imagination, how it is transactive, a factory of simulacra, a secret seam between what has passed and what is yet to come. The extraordinary richness of this book lies in its showcasing of language as a worthy opponent in wrestling the giant of time; how a phrase, even a phoneme can lock as well as set time free, how poetry can contend with the eternal and the sudden, how the lyric can subdue time's machinations with a pulse all its own: chiming, colliding or stilled at will— "I am free to fill the silence with denser silence," the poet declares—a triumph for us all.

—Shadab Zeest Hashmi, author of *Ghazal Cosmopolitan*

"This is not about a clock at all but what the clock surrounds" —time is in the center of this extraordinary poetry collection by Endi Bogue Hartigan, who drives us (through a kind of incantatory speech) into a world of subversive syntax, of compressed and expanded language and, most of all, of meaning. This "apparatus," as the poet subtly refers to the compositions on these pages, rearranges the outlines of matter versus organic matter, of the objective versus the subjective in our known (and unknown) spaces, giving them a new range of expression, a new clarity, to signify and bridge. These poems connect the molecular to the universal to the public to the personal in a single breath. It's a wildly original and ingenious book, but what catapults us into the bliss of this reading is a sense of finding (astonished) the "arrows and notches" of our earthly human print.

—Flávia Rocha, author of *Exosfera*

Elegies and hour entries, foxes and orchids, revolving and recurring contemplations of once, never, always—the nature of time and our existence with and within time, within a system of time that foments "worry hordes," "|anotherAmericannumber|," "|nebulanation|," "|lightlet|"... Swirling with condensations and collisions of language, observations, societal and personal conditions, at the center of which abides a constantly fervently spinning heart, these poems also ask: "Can the clock burn?" I think the clock does burn in these poems, also morphs and contracts and grows second (and third, fourth, other) second-hands, seeks alternate ways of counting, amplifying and expanding time inside the interstices that nest beneath and beyond what we can count, what we can comprehend. These poems are clocks of their own count and their own making, setting their tiny pulses against our current collective sense of an impending clock, to dream and create their own intricate, delicate music and meter and measure of what it means to be and feel at this particular moment in time.

—Dao Strom, author/songwriter of *Instrument/Traveler's Ode*

I am awed by Endi Bogue Hartigan's ability to inhabit time's perplexities. Her sonically sensitive and wondrous meditations on continuity and chronology, accumulation and containment, contemplate the "measure of measure," each one finding a different way to mesmerize time to investigate its constructions. Never have I so intimately felt the bewilderment of being "off the clock" and of the clock. I love *oh orchid o'clock*'s quality of deep prayer, how it attends intimately to the feeling of time in lived experience, how it lets go of instrumentality to consider the instrument.

—Mary Szybist, author of *Incarnadine*

Cover art by Thérèse Murdza, acrylic color and pencil on canvas
untitled 08-1822 (i love how you know the roses)

Interior typeface: Adobe Jenson Pro and Cronos Pro
Cover and interior design by Endi Bogue Hartigan and Laura Joakimson


"Letter in April: IV" (three-line excerpt) by Inger Christensen, translated by Susanna Nied,
from LIGHT, GRASS, & LETTER IN APRIL, copyright ©1979 by Inger Christensen. Translation
copyright © 2011 by Susanna Nied. Reprinted by permission of
New Directions Publishing Corp.


Library of Congress Cataloging-in-Publication Data

Names: Hartigan, Endi Bogue, author.
Title: oh orchid o'clock / Endi Bogue Hartigan.
Description: Oakland, California : Omnidawn Publishing, 2023. | Summary:
"This book speaks the language of clock-sense as a living instrument,
exposing the sensory impacts of our obsession with time. This work's
interwinding lyrics move through histories as a nervous system moves. In
that body we hear this text sound out the maternal and the material as
if played by fingers along the frets of meaning. We hear the poems
reveal how we let our days become over-clocked and over-transactional
and over-weaponed. This instrument pleads, records, nursery-rhymes, and
notches sonically, investigating what it is to be close to time:
collective time with its alarms and brutalities, and bodily time,
intricate and familial. How can we be captured in systems of measure and
be complicit with them, how can we be breaking from them, creating them,
and immune to them? Clock gears press against interconnecting
systems-economic/capitalist, astronomical, medical, governmental,
fantastical-where even language is a measure or prayer that takes off
the face of the clock and exposes its springs and weights"
-- Provided by publisher.

Identifiers: LCCN 2022057615 | ISBN 9781632431158 (trade paperback)
Subjects: LCSH: Time--Poetry. | LCGFT: Poetry.
Classification: LCC PS3608.A78725 O38 2023 | DDC 811/.6--dc23/eng/20221212
LC record available at https://lccn.loc.gov/2022057615


Published by Omnidawn Publishing, Oakland, California
www.omnidawn.com
10 9 8 7 6 5 4 3 2 1
ISBN: 978-1-63243-115-8

# oh orchid o'clock

Endi Bogue Hartigan

OMNIDAWN PUBLISHING
OAKLAND, CALIFORNIA
2023

—to Patrick and Jackson

# Contents

"A caring
 like what is needed
 to repeat the world...."

—Inger Christensen, tr. by Susanna Nied

## I'm talking about their rotation

—The predictable commencement of annual flooding of the Nile River is said to have formed the foundation of the ancient Egyptian calendar. Calculations were made using nilometers, vertical water-measurement devices, influencing taxation, crop planning, and more.

*I'm talking about the black cows in the pasture along the highway between here and the office: some days the black cows' snouts are pointed in the same direction in the morning and the opposite direction in the evening, all 200-300 or so, parallel dipping their snouts; some days they are helter-skelter; some days the shadows are crisp some days the shadows are swallowed but they have shadows on all days; and the wet eyes of the cows have an angle with which they lean into the wet grass, so they are a kind of dial to themselves and their light, visible to themselves or not. I might be comforted driving by saying cow shadow o'clock, saying east black cow o'clock, I might be comforted by talking about their rotation.*

/it is child eyelash o'clock /it is having to look o'clock it is
Nile flood o'clock /it is percolate o'clock

/it is morning birds plus socket sound of car closing /21st century pastoral
o'clock it is flashflood fear o'clock /it is TV van at the shooting site rim

/it is miscount of the dead o'clock
/it is remember to call remember to call find a corner to make a call o'clock

/it is the blue jay screech o'clock /it is having to look o'clock
/it is innocent eyelash o'clock /it is the clock continuing despite

o'clock /people emptying from their eyes
/it is yesterday's rose-dew o'clock

/it is tearing the work blouse off its hanger o'clock /it is
tearing and not /it is that blouse again that headline again it is

everything I forgot creeping up in tides
/it is people split and swelled

confiding overflow o'clock /it is the shadow of a gun /the shadow of
the cow o'clock /it is what is allowed in the shadow

/it is the president's turned up o'clock it is America's deadliness and dailiness
o'clock /it is glued to the headline o'clock

it is lunchhour-beeline o'clock /it is it's only Tuesday o'clock another
curbside memorial o'clock another caterpillar miracle o'clock another

people emptying from their lives o'clock or into their
lives o'clock the Nile floods the Nile floods every hotspell in this week

/it is child-wake, it is flood of what's at stake o'clock,
/it is the morning rupture the American rupture that

shadow-bleeds and swells /it is the felling of the shadow o'clock
/I'm talking about the black cows.


**hour entry:** *Speech has little*

*Speech has little to do with it, ultimately, or speech has everything to do with it, or odd,
people turning into speech clusters, or speech is a kind of nursery rhyme to God.*

**hour entry:** *Gyms are Thanksgivings for clocks*

Gyms are Thankgivings for clocks, because people are only there for so long and there is the question of economy which is a mathematical relation to the consumption of their lives. I dress in a women's locker room in which you must be 13 at least to be, so it is a post-pubescent locker room and the women speak frankly as they dress.

Listen: there is a prayer to speak less or less mathematically than speech. I speak about the elliptical clock-count, the 30-minute sign up, I endeavor not to speak of prayer charts but they exist too consumed by marigolds and sheets. They are consumed in being legible to God so the moment I utter something it is written in the ether log onto them and at the same moment vanishes, I hope, received.

I can't tell you how grateful I am for this erasure.

**I'm up early scanning worries**

/the clock is maternal and infernal and torn
/I'm up early scanning worries /how many mothers worry

in early morning hordes, how many worry by lifting
useless familiar material their hands can feel:

the dried up moon-gold gourd from last October
or the October before /how many worry in the forms

of their spinal cords /one nugget at a time
one pinch without the whole snaking instrument
that holds them up /this child is running
in the dark running by the reservoir in the dark and there is nothing
to worry about /repeat repeat
pinpricks of stars, galactic nicks and plucks
/the dark is the absence of light the dried gourd
is the evaporated gourd /I can lift the emptiness of worry

and sense the air can feel the evaporation having occurred and the perfect
moon-gold warted instrument of the vegetable.

**second entries:** |slickarticle|

|slickarticle||verticaltrust||paperclipwe||cubicleapple|
|slipapple||adverbialheart||wearelitwe||seedamongseed|

**hour entry:** *that water beasts like shaky beliefs*

*That water beasts have undulating backs with serrated fins at the top, carved intricately to the tip, and that the elaborate wooden planets and moons and visible gear notches of 16th century astrolabes attempted to mirror this. That headlines are not repeated merely though they repeat at Tuesday's tip, today's reported shooting is not remembered or repeated merely, I can read and reread headlines, I can sense the undeniable quivering lip on a screen, and cannot instrumentally not follow that lip and shake.*

**hour entry:** *All bells must hold all clocks*

*The clock's etymological root being "clocca" being bell, a nerve root shivering roundness, a medieval prayer alarm, a cradling sound shell. The bell a striking into the temporal then a tidepool retraction, the bell an oscillating fraction of the friction of continuance, pulling water instance out and out and out.*

**to be inserted early into the unwound clock**

/paper reins so only the strength of paper can direct the horse only
the slightest tug

only the earliest entry
*mangled screen door, faucet whir*

we swirled and ran to get to *la-la* we were one-tenth of ourselves, late,
if I am not here on the page where am I *with*

*the spatula stir, the flat nose of the tool*
only the slightest dragon if you overstate yourselves you

are slightly unforgiven


/paper reins so only the strength of paper can direct the horse only
the slightest tug

only the don't-be-cranky-mom sentry
*pat the mane, flying fur*

we were facing deadlines racing we were one-tenth of ourselves, spent
if I am not here on the page where am I *with*

*the carpool weather talk mistakes spilled gym-locks clunking*
/only the slightest penciled goose-flock if you yourself are something spilled

something spilling
loose then caught, a signature to authorize, a barbed wire knot


/paper reins so only the strength of paper can direct the horse only
the slightest tug

only the backdoor buzz entry
*stamped mail, coughing fire*

/we were facing morning email compression we were one-tenth of ourselves,
lent to pixelated e-report if I am not here on the page where am I *with*

*the barely leafed strawberry* this is how you draw a dragon
*only virtual worlds break*

if you yourself are something swelled with
stream-breath, draw the dragon as a horse continually pulled from

present tense, yourself the sensed rider.

**second entries:** |insertinsect|

|insertinsect||seesomethingin||tinfoilballall||lastcalltalk|
|throughthrow||silverwingy||unalivehe||breathedhewalked|

**hour entry:** *"Calendaring" is a verb.*

*"Calendaring" is a verb. You can "clock yourself in." These terms like rows of hothouse orchids living in some God-forsaken pre-purchase interval steam. New verbs for new measures, new signs of transaction as home, this noon hour spent "off the clock," but spent entirely on calendaring alone, appointments blocked, lab tests graphed, orders tracked, this noon hour packed in screen-time and foam, this stem of the orchid holding itself up as an orchid. You can even check off "orchid," you can list, for Tuesday, "unnatural hothouse mixture of purple and green."*

**hour entry:** *When John Adams wrote*

*Another toll, another count of automatic weapon casualties, another occasion of America losing track of its math. I read today that when John Adams wrote "Thirteen Clocks were made to Strike together," clocks were a tolling of public event, rung, an occasion or station in sun. I slept, and woke, I slept too long and woke. I tried to count the measured world by reading. Read "Thirteen Clocks," read the late morning sun slant, read the current count outpaces past casualty counts, read "Just three percent of adults own half of America's guns." Something automatic in measure, too automatic. I woke out of 9.25 hours of sleep I calculated automatically upon waking. I saw a crow out the window that was the occasion of a crow pecking frozen specks. I read the headlines leaking into headlines, saw the orchid opal sky calculating nothing. I have an inclination to stream and I don't know what it means today. I have an inclination to lie in my husband's shoulder crook and let the day snowdrift let the dimness become wide, so a shoulder is a kind of stream too. The argument is made that the streaming of time is a perception trick. The argument is made that we have moved past occasion to incremental measure that we are obsessed with measure and stricken. I have an inclination to obsessively stream, to arise and move not through incremental measures of occasion but through water. The early clocks were water clocks but it was shown that water was imprecise, was subject to pressure and pore—even streams of consciousness can encounter ducts and brim. I am conscious of my husband's warmth because of more than his warmth. Do not mistake headlines for measure. We were held in God's soft pocket. Do not mistake automatic grieving for water.*

**you be the woodcutter**

/there were more of us than I could count in the clock, more notches, shifts,
triggers, more misaligned stream, I asked for foxes to appear
in between our footsteps, I asked for someone to draw wider leaves
between the alarms of the lilies, before they closed up.

*you be the woodcutter I'll be the waterwheel*
*you be the crescent moon I'll be the III trio*
*you be electric I'll be particulate*
*you be the pendulum you be the Sun*

/there were more of us in water clocks, more in violent time-held streams,
more than once, a child, I slipped my body into the tooth of a blowhole
and stood there as the coolness rose, the water surface rose,
swirled to the brink of anything held, more of us than water wells.

*you be the clockface I'll be the flatness*
*you be the pendulum I'll be the weight*
*you be the fingerprint I'll be the windknob*
*you be the off/on you be the Sun*

/between the actual notches I thought if I could find /between
the 20-point headline /X dead /trigger moon /school shooting X fled
/if I could find /between the sieving disbelief the ring and tick I thought
/if I could X out the most actual miniscule nicks of present love.

*you be the cuckoo bird I'll be the finial*
*you be the waterwheel I'll be the spring*
*you be the southern VI I'll be the night ticks*
*you be the orangewood you be the Sun*

/every hour there was a melody inserted in which time stretched
into a spell in which the cuckoo bird emerged and the kids
would run to it, clamber up the sofa to see the wooden bird
emerge, and stand tiptoed, unstable, inside the melody.

**I still the clock.**

/I still the clock.

/I still the clock by holding the pendulum coin still so that
the mechanism stops
and I can sleep without the consciousness of it.

to still the clock is a ritual of the demagnification of clocks.

/it is a kind of violence of fiction for the clock to not
function as a clock while others click and breathe and blink.

the eyes blink more before they stop functioning as eyes.

/the rapid eye movement of dream frightening being pure
pulse, pure frenetic zag force

/to watch a gold-painted platinum extravagant clock you're an excess you're
a fire you're in competition with the tiredness of time.
/to hold in your satiny eyelids the still unstill pendulum of
the gaudy machination you are in unison

with the aspirant expirations of the day.

**second entries:** |bobbypinaccumulate|

|bobbypinaccumulate||lostauntseason||Christmastimecrimerate|
|eyeshadownomenclature||gethomeget||sickallweekfaint|
|Santapinksaint||knickknackprayercup||restuprestup|
|listwhatyouwantits||*thisthisthisthis*||kissedcoolforehead|

**say never and never**

/say never and never is in the clock
/never is an approximation
exterior to the clock so it is a liability to the clock
and must be represented as a fox there

/the clockhands never move together they pass as sidewalk walkers
by each not seeing each other continually
/the foxtails look like fox tails except don't disappear like the animal

/try to state anything never, say:
I never thought I would have such love, or,
/He never had a place to sleep, or
They never thought it would happen here

/what you say as a continual field forming with foxes, live ones in the clock
dashing and disrupting
/say the clock spins around the never, not a fluke /the moment said
it is there on the page with impossible-to-remove blackberry juice

/say it was follicled with dust, then punctured, then black water sprayed
/my life sprayed from what it wasn't in the field,
a kind of feathering at the cusp like grass meets sea

/I was tethered as a clockhand or a grassspear
I was finned and fanned
by the instrument, but the fox was not tethered to the blackberry stain,
so let the chasing clutch of clockhands be.

**hour entry:** *Believe in fluke*

*There's a clock shop on Stark Street across from the tax man. There, a stamp of
bodily space time on each receipt. If you are broke, you have to believe in
out-calculating or out-lucking the clock, believe in nicks of time or fluke, if you're
broke or broke again, if the clock is a function of a system you are barely in, if
|grocerycalculation||dilutedmilk||delayedcheckstand|, if you insert the debit card
and wait in tilting tension toward the machine.*

## once the clock is stilled

/once the clock is stilled, the creatures come
out of domestic fields.

/to the southwest of the extension of the beak
is the horseshoe /a child decorated the horseshoe
with mock gems and paint so that it is no other horseshoe.

the gems in the horseshoe say the arrangement of gems make the gems.

/they don't speak they reflect nothing they are
superfluous as mountains and we were in awe of them.

**hour entry:** *I made a chart today a beautiful*

*I made a chart today a beautiful weekly chart for links and breakages and shoulder
pulls and astronaut walks. Some items are measured in repetitions, some in minutes
and I endeavor to note on which days I have devoted my body's minutes and repeated
movements through time space onto this chart. At the end I hope for late endorphin
states, and an even gait, and for uncertain ailments to dissipate by my discipline.*

**hour entry:** *Here is a school bus moving through the pink dawn*

*Here is a school bus moving through the pink dawn. The bus is an arm on a clock moving in a circuitous circle through its route, advancing toward the school bell. It is abruptly light here at 7am because today we moved the clockhands back, spring-forward-fall-back, a task the collective tactic of a past war. When World War I occasioned a need to save coal, Germany responded by adjusting the dawn, and daylight-saving was born, other governments mimicked form, though today the reasons shift |spectralraft||markettassle|. The arrow is nearly weightless, pushed, even the return feels faintly wrong, pinned in place by mnemonic device. I am not saying the bus in daylight lacks happiness, the school bus hisses and clacks, but even the pinkest light can lack continuous accuracy, unspooling.*

**second entries:** |trajectoryfactory|

|trajectoryfactory||facthissing||casualtylivestream||spiralorangepeel|
|staycoil||couragemess||lessquill||vacuumwheel||*Ifeelfine*|

## the longest hour is the shortest

/the longest hour is the shortest too where you are merely an eye
|anttime||circleconstruction|

in the longest hour there was |wetantpetal||fiddlepanic|
|anotherAmericannumber|

/unimaginable shootings occurred every several days and the hour
absorbed them
/the longest hour a crack in time |largelargerheadlines|

/the longest hour /a nesting doll in which smaller hours arose out of
the flowered tight belly of the hour with complete /specific lives

/whose thin-skin nasturtium whose sister whose license
/absorb I can't
I can't remember the hour exactly, only hours that nested in or from it

whose |headlineligature||petalwrinkled||lastwordword|
/I cleaned to absorb what I hadn't heard /how I can admire the ant's industry
then mop its route industriously
what an hour is to an ant, what a second is to an automatic weapon
|Xdead||9dead||shooterdead| nauseous reading

/what grief is through a list /what an hour is to God's kiss
/miscounted at first

/the longest hour made headlines into eruptions
/made strangers into cousins

may we love all strangers more
|hellowetnasturtium||largelargerheadlines|


**second entries:** |waitasecondpheasant|

|waitasecondpheasant||tameyourbraintosleep||ricegrainsameness|
|formsofformless||stormscheme||*waitasecI*||crytickcrytalk|
|identicalpadlock||losttracklate||nebulanation||*waitwillyouwait*|

**hour entry:** *The locker room women have sore arms*

The locker room women have sore arms from lifting babies, and immunizations for travel and cysts awaiting analysis. The clock is a voyeur that does not know their children's names, or, the source of certain sleeve stains, the way the paper lists an inmate's charges. I should not be speaking of them here, except to say on Thursday after workouts that lotion is my lotion too, I love that brand, it's a feat some days to be bare and muted.

**hour entry:** *There were more of us*

There were more of us in worry hordes, more bleeds in time than I could count. I worry that I have bled beyond the marigold blur yellow burned to red, bled beyond my stamen math or snapped my personhood hinge or that worries also were corrupted beyond measure. The clock is leaking brutal exaction from its sutures and in the missed calculations of these leaks—forms bows envelope stacks surgical incisions ballots clauses tent flaps—all that I am not keeping up with—subtract that, and you have the lava-bled red of the marigold stitch.

## the cuckoo before it emerges

the cuckoo before it emerges, the cuckoo in the dark wormhole
of the clock /the closer I live to it the closer I must live to it

/a discerning hope in which I hope the pond comes clear
/to the cuckoo it is dark except for the moment observance turns toward it

/I started to imagine the actions before the election
/I started to imagine the cuckoo before observance

/I started making ceramic foxes. I always liked the shape of
fantastical foxes. I started a kickboxing class today.
I started signing more petitions. I started waterwheeling want.
I started making waterwheels without the water knowing.
/what did I wheel?
/It's a lonely thing to start, to feel

/to chute out of darkness, start and stop
/the sculpted creatures emerge and toll
/petitions folded into virtual petitions

/heart I tricked into something shaped like a fox or a petition or a mole
/a jellylike spider bead made brief appearances in the cuckoo clock hole

/to the cuckoo it is dark except for the melodic emergence of the world
/the melody rides off other melodies so skews in the chute

/before observance, before material measure before election notch and scissor
something starts, barely, uncurls
half-recognizable /I think the orangewood is starting to erode,
I think the melody is listening, non-transactional and old

/before any orangewood, before the quickening of darkness and field

**second entries:** |ohgoodness|

|ohgoodness||textdove||entirelyinlove||bonestructuremath|
|babyblanketfur||dandelionshe||thisguyhe|

## some questions about temporal government

what is not a clock in this house /is the imported eraser-less gnawed #2 pencil the
tiny bent metallic bucket at the pencil tip a clock /is the beloved crawdad J. and
M. caught, sloshed home on a Saturday from Blue Lake a clock /is the metallic
goldfish knickknack a gift from a past boss's China trip 20 years back a clock /what
work day is not the first workday I ever worked as a kid the strangeness of time
being clocked /what first paycheck to a poor kid is not a wound knob /what 10
fingers are not a clock /I'm counting to ten with a toddler /is the toddler toddling
a clock /what rotting tangerine is not a clock's lung /what policy bucket /is a
president's term a clock /is empire /is a fake raindrop recorded on a cell phone app
/is the forgotten childgame making strawberries talk a clock /is a jinx /is a skipped
meal /is a stained sink /does the clock dance /is the pain of empires clocked /is
the vertical chain of the cuckoo /is the vertical growth of wealth /is the rooftop /is
the sinking rooftop /what is not a clock in the crawdad /what is not a translucent
instrument of instruments /is J. coming home at 3 or 4 /who is picking up whom
today /is the see-through pinkish skeletal fabric home /what is not expiring from
its gear from its policy from its prayer from its body /is government for or of /does
love destroy clocks /what is not a crawdad caught digging itself in and out of tiny
rocks /*what what what*

**hour entry:** *all galaxies are not clocks*

*All galaxies are not clocks. In the bluntness of mass violence news, all light is oversaid right now. I shut my eyes and spun in argument. I apologized to the clock for not being present, I apologized to no one in particular in basement dim |underwaterheart| |lungspeechfight||galacticfallflock|. Why should I walk upstairs to lit time at all, to what the clock must point to? Overlit wicks, planetary eye-tones of the injured, their collisions, every lifted stretcher every bruised orchid spirit oversaid or unprotected or too ungently held. This is not just about closeness to the forward leak of clocks that can only move forward have no choice but to notch and notch and notch and not desist.*

*If I dismantled the wind knob. If I peeled off the clock-hands of the clock |fingernailtear||industrialpetal||Madonnaspinestalk|. If I snap off the clock hands, if I slice my fingerprint-finger, bending and snapping off the clock hands, leaving the bare white face of the clock, the galaxy would still contain this knocking around.*

**second entries:** |barrettemetal|

|barrettemetal||settleworry||funeralwear||andherbrain||mirrorfissure| |prayertattle||MRIcradle||Saturnringfair||andherquery||airingprayer|

## someone was throwing away a chandelier

/someone was throwing away a chandelier
on the curb side /a heap of chandelier parts in the grass of the curbside

/the instrument a kind of dusty faux gold crustacean,
an 8-legged industrial crab, barnacle-fluted, embossed,

bent lily-socketed, overlaid with chains,
a grotesque heap of decorative loot

/it was tempting to want to gently kick, or lift it up to see
|lamenttent||reactionwrought| /to carry the cankered creature of it

home hanging from my wrists, to be a strained makeshift ceiling, making sure
it didn't swing too hard and scrape me, swaying, splay out its coiling veins

/be somehow less than grasp by grasping it, tempting to crave torrential rain
on the sidewalk, neck-slick, to downpour-talk or tide-lisp and I

/was information-tired, wired with update and accumulate, replaying news feeds
in my brain /searching automatically for them, untame, neural-

laced to the carapace |miscountfont||pricetagfest||electionfervor|
/I was tempted to take anyone with me by the wrist,

take the data weather of a person by the narrow of the wrist,
take any coagulated speech cluster of a receiving person,

take diagnoses, receipts, eyelashes of the dead, soiled sleeves,
by the thin of the wrist, walk 8 or 8000 blocks together, whatever it takes,

to enter, gather beneath or amidst some upside down tidefroth test,
beneath its event of barely consequential light

/it might be dark in this room.
I might be held by its lapse.

I might have a chandelier like nobody lighting nothing but this
|wetfusetether||embeddedarm||diminvitationforever|

## 23 clocks and instruments of removal

—after taking snapshots of all the clocks in my life on a single workday

/3 minutes to say good morning to my son
3 minutes good morning (*have a good day*
*I love*—) /the removal of myself
in the blank clock-like eye of the dove

/the clocks I don't know to be clocks respond
/distracted, aloof, or soothed by the ticking
/a dove without clocks,
an infant blink, clockless

/a personal email sent for no reason
(I talked to removal, the hovering arm)

*/instruments for dropping*
*instruments in water,*
*dropping one world to another*

*a kind of pigeon gurgling musical,*
*an outdated family photo*
*framed in an office cubicle*

/here's where the cuckoo bird comes
/here's where the interstice,
here's where the sun

(I think I'll call Patrick just to talk)—
/the clock that starts when day arrives
/the clock that starts when love starts—
the arrival of the person to the clock

*/instruments that fail to fail:*
*office corner clocks, knitting needles,*

*hummingbird feeders, AR-15s, sestinas,*
*headlines, institutions sometimes*
*fail to fail, fail to leak*
*from themselves*


(& people were quiet at work)
/& no one would let someone talk
at that meeting /jets overhead—
too low causing alarm

/& pigeons send gurgles like emails
/no one responds between seconds but canyons
/dove v. pigeon, clocked time v. given

/I talked to myself between emails
/the removal of little blue pills

/I talk to him continually anyway
which means segues from ticking or not
/which means loving as protesting clocks (overrun)


*/instruments for dropping*
*doves from past doves,*
*days from past days, or one particular*
*dove from another on telephone wire*

*a kind of paperdoll chainlink,*
*in which cloning and sequencing blur*


/the inappropriate comment at a meeting
/frozen stir
/the clock of immediate reaction by
compensatory laughter

/the impersonal nature of time caught
in the personal context of clocks,

standardized or not (talk, respond)
/the division of persons into heartbeats

/the clock of the 6pm news theme song
/the Ariel Disney mermaid clock with
water-like water drops
/the 5:00 clatter, the reason to stay

/the overtime eligible position
/the empty chatter in office kitchens

> /instruments babies play with, little
> neon rattles, all innocence
> stand in a circle: the words
> hysterical & clerical & miracle

/I didn't know what to say at the time
then later I thought
of the perfect response

/a ticking under your skin v.
a gurgling that's soothingly loud

/clocks as only clocks: the dove for doves,
the clock for clocks, the removal of the clock
in the blank clock-like eye of the dove

/the form of hitting mute to talk,
/the clock that starts when pigeons start moving
Ok *see you later*, ankles of crowds

> /instruments that suggest scarring,
> gists of form, merely:
> gauze, for example,
> curdles, trout skin, white sails

/cuckoo cuckoo! then the wooden villagers spin
then a boy runs to see it
a boy runs to see it again

/turn the corner
and it's right there
/you should know your position
/you should know how to talk by now

(I get to see Patrick at 6)
/I'm off the clock or on the clock
/the removal of nothing, the addition of computing


*/a blunt instrument that untalks,*
*untells, gathering future nursery rhymes,*
*quantum nations unsinging routine muting,*
*military fly-bys, cockle shells*


/I'll tell you what happened this morning:
the clock of the hollow red school bell
/I called to tell you,

I called for no reason
/all bells were clocks, and started and stopped
/the removal of the phone from the ear


**hour entry:** *In Milwaukie, in 1908*

*The middles of time make all time hazard. That jewelers advertise out-of-reach gems*
*with clocks. That if I dismantled the clock I would dismantle talking softly to my*
*family against lost time. That in Milwaukie, in 1908, a mayor ordered the destruction*
*of "hazards" on city streets including signs, placards, and jewelers' clocks, ordered*
*firefighters in the deep of night to dismantle the street clocks as if they were ads, merely,*
*which they were, but their destruction drew public fury, and the street clocks became*
*endowed with something marrowed and carried.*

**hour entry:** *At least three times last week*

At least three times last week, I broke the time space agreement and the squealing of interplanetary railroads began.

At least three times I was not prompt. I was two minutes late for the vanpool and I was left in the pay-day check parking lot and had to drive my weary form to work stitching the speedometer to my eyelids. I overcompensated reacting to the timing of a coming car and thumped my car into the rearview mirror of a parked car and snapped it. I fell asleep in the vanpool and when I woke, part of me was with the time-spent foxes still in the drugged traffic field and I left the laptop under the seat. My cell phone was in the past fingerprint of the present Korean factory worker, my heart was in the double yellow parallels drifting from present to past from task to task being overspent on promptness.

The only solution was to stay in one place until rotations had resolved. The only solution was to crawl into something pure and round pure and round like a pearl or like the magma core without instrumentation and interrelation curlage.

## the nemesis of all clocks

/water, all forms of water,
corroding water, leveling, mirroring and suffocating and suctioning
and people cannonballing every summer in and in and in
/not the cuckoo clock waterwheel, exactly, but what it fails

*I failed to even get to _____ at the hospital.*
*I failed to even feel the marigold shift gold, Heraclitus' ever shift, missed.*
*I was too distracted or worried or overtired.*
*I failed to tell gunfire from backfire.*

/so sense misfired, so people being too close to the swallow-swell
of the wave to see the gargantuan marble green incision
/too close to certain given streams
of violence to see violence /I'm talking about the most naïve silken seashell
wish of the clock, its close and closer knobs and pinions and triggers and pivots
to tinker and knock
on the pressurized protest of water, to harness itself to its nemesis:
the skull slap the undertow, the instance flow as
dragon eye flashing green /the waterwheel on the cuckoo clock
an attempt to half-sync the instrument to the matter of its undoing, to sparse it
out in bucket drops and in doing so to be able to live
as close as possible to the rapids |rapideyemovement||repeatheadlinesno|
|bucketstow||shetalkedtoagates||flagswavestay|

/Hello, I love you /the wettest word is day

## hour entry: *It is reported*

*It is reported that 11th century Chinese peoples employed a wooden clocklike*
*instrument that calibrated time by burning camphor, rhubarb, aromatic scents through*
*a labyrinth of gradations in the wood. Knowing the recipe for particular incense and*
*the particular mapped incineration path of freshest ash, one could map the hour of*
*day… it is Mountain Pear o'clock, it is Pine Ball it is Maze Petal it is Spine Curl*
*o'clock, only partial days were sensed, only part of this is imagined.*

**hour entry:** *On the other hand I was complicit*

*On the other hand I was complicit in the instrument. I was privileged to work a work day and I loved to lose myself in work, work like hell toward a deadline and be spent in it, whirl through the liquid hour and come out the other side of the hour devoid of anything but what was produced by the thieving focus of the incremental fiction of the hour. Loved the emptying service and the bottomless canyon of work, the arrows and notches and memos in which it takes everything to move a gear and be a gear, quiver doubt and tendons in the neck giving out and half-implemented policy and Himalayan daydream-fare, the swallow and steal of deadline, all-quill or pink-toil or self-spell, if I managed well I was left in soil, where fearful lack of clock would disappear, the absence did not matter, I would be a notch in the waterwheel and feel it lift the water.*

**second entries:** |NewYearsbaby|

|NewYearsbaby||firstbeforefirst||quiverlipsundial||continuitytipped|
|restartsundrip||*IsaidI'dcall*||*diddiddid*||reforgeforward||cordandcrylit|

**hour entry:** *This noon*

This noon is your noon: decisively. Before we had our standard times we had regional times generally agreed to by the commerce of a railroad line. Noon means noon, so that we can walk in space and time and sell each other steam machines and huckleberry jam. I dreamed too realistically of my own death and woke damp and spooked. No one agrees on the time of their death. We agree on this. I dreamed I walked till noon wore off. I disagree with my dream but I want my feet to keep moving in the moss-softness of it.

**hour entry:** *This noon is your noon*

This noon is your noon: decisively. I disagree with my noon on the basis that I call it mine.

## my superhero is made of crunched-up chandeliers

/chandeliers in the blood of
the peripheral heart, catching residual threat

/don't ask to see the grip of time, crystallizing,
don't ask for light to drip in one direction

/little fists release their grip, infant fists,
the fingers small as matches,
/see everything caught in time can uncatch, you

can pray continually if you can precede clock-tick /ask

/immunity from ashes, immunity from asking against
and again the coolness of the ashes
/ask /ask

/see everything that catches outside of the hive-head
is slowed for a split second in the light so that slow conscience
has a kick start, and the bee changes direction

/no, you can't give others that art you can't ask for
superheroes to start praying /start over

/chandeliers made of crunched-up chandeliers /capes made
of bee-stingers quivering over pansy-fields unused

/no singlefield no single
super-villain, the castle drips with intricate internal threat but it is an
overfamiliar sea or a trickle or less

/I was dressed in less than a cape I was not empty but I felt
the space in myself, and light

/lightbulbs made of living thumb-sized doves that swallow
gargantuous planet-sadnesses swallow them whole as light where
no one gives up, no one gives
those doves up

/up with the numinous heroes, up and up, they will have antennae

masked as cobwebs strung between lit
corners that sense the presence of infant grips, loved

/light organs, porous hope so that

/ *a hive is a castle is an organ is a being, safe, and lit,*
*safe, and lit*
/anywhere you are you can slip into it

**second entries:** |feedthechildrenfeedthelake|

|feedthechildrenfeedthelake||throughthemilkI||filteredmorning|
|barelyreefed||dailyroute||muteleaf||purezephyred|
|strawberrylord||redsieve||gdmorningleaf||warninglift|

**hour entry:** *Start the stopwatch. The animal was a light fixture, no the animal was a shovel*

*Start the stopwatch. The animal was a light fixture, no the animal was a shovel, no the animal was the industry of pocket-watches and light fixtures and shovels. The animal was Frederick Winslow Taylor performing industrial time studies of other men in a factory shoveling. The animal crawled into the people and they crawled into the animal daily. The people in the animal go home to actual animals, Labradors, and Kool-Aid colored parakeets and heart-full children and their hearts are soft as oysters soft as suture leaks soft as lost time, forgotten weeks. Stop.*

*Start the stopwatch. There was light in the factory late, late, and Frederick Winslow Taylor held a stopwatch in the late 20th century factory light. Frederick Winslow Taylor held a stopwatch and started and stopped it to men shoveling, to arrive at the most efficient method to industrialize factory-time. The privilege to crawl into the animal was an economic privilege to hold the industry of light or time in the animal shoveling. The stopwatch had a mechanical heart and it was more dependable than any palpitation it cut through. But this is only where the study starts, because the animals turn inside out daily and emerged from stopwatch cocoons. The moths flutter into light as faux home. Children can be depended upon to have their own clocks. Frederick Winslow Taylor could be depended on to appear, looking backward, as a heart made of cuttlefish bone. The parakeets pecking cuttlefish bone appeared to peck at pale hearts and the pecking kept their beaks sharp. Stop.*

## magnetic calendar

the organization of being while being we need
a family magnetic calendar to keep track /*oh what today*

*now what now who?*
domesticity: how people carry it into their cubicles and cars
/Tupperware splayed date bars and picture frames and one is famous

for her date bars /they are afraid of becoming vehicles
but there are certain types of engines you must trust enough to drive

with the others through virtual trainings bomb-scare-backpacks
office dings ER check-ins God kabooms grasshopper straw-wings

*which day is today?* /people carrying their laptops everywhere
custom screens /you gasp behind the door

you are dreaming something
that makes you gasp behind the door


**hour entry:** *And what about the hoarders*

*And what about the hoarders who seem to protest clocks, fill the gaps with what they're not? The collector of doll parts, the woman with 62 cats, the man with every newspaper of his life, stacked by date carefully, the collector of medicinal brown flasks lined up for mere glow. Nearly identical incomplete stories reported in the news, repeatedly, like children painting rainbows after rainbows.*

**hour entry:** *That it never*

—That in 1751 Carolus Linnaeus conceived of a floral clock, a botanical garden designed with species that blossomed predictably at certain hours of day, so that walking through it, one could tell time from the petals.

*That it never worked may have been critical to the pollen of future ruins and revolts, that the lily wrist opacity decided not to show itself, that 6:00 industry was lost to the ants and the nectar chambers, that I got nothing intended done all day and coworkers floated between cubicle sunbeams, that the cockle shell women and the snapdragon breaths and the pin code clues and the politicians' shoes never quite stood to stand there in a punctuating sequence, that all sequence would stymy and revolt, that Mary Mary, alarm and delay and caterpillar-staring, that the empirical battalion of the flower clock disintegrated by noon, that subsequently there would be wildernesses of soon and soon and soon where the ruins of the instrument held us.*

**second entries:** |potholehotline|

|potholehotline||anticipatecoral||automationnation|pinpointprayerjoint|
|almostthere||fearabacus||goldentorn||maternalcopernicus|

## symptoms of camellias

if (God) I have to tether, re-tether to minute-grip continually
/I watch the orbit, watch for signs of it

/watch the sidewalk, watch the magazines leak ads,
a space-watch ad in *Popular Science* /the topography of time-space

slips from watch /I watch the crows watching asphalt
/not a knife-beak, not an ink fluke /the pressure of watching time

leaks or darts or curls /if it's a crow's flat eye an orbit's cry
a pulp glistening /fish-lines glisten

being thrown /if it's the shape of a net /of a sieve /of unspent love
/if time as a thrown fish-line or a pulp-nodule

/the tangerine pillow /and in each leakage, each liquid node of light,
an ink-crow advertising blot /time, forsakenness

of any sculpt of time /the lines swaying power-line segments
/if they do not sway

/time to want and throw modeled wants /the slope of time
as a compressed eardrum /an internal tension in the flying comet
/*it's time to check the time*

/if 17 missed texts reported on my screen was not a prime number I
would trust it less /if the rest of the day

from the sofa is spent describing symptoms of
camellias it is called guessing pink-speed /I want a space-watch with

shivery digits /I want the same flowers as you, but moving.


**second entries:** |sdwhereyougoing?|

|*sdwhereyougoing?*||owingdream||nomilkwalk||screendoorclatter||hi!matter|
|wrinkledollar||sd*Iloveyou*||forcedfence||debtdance||barelyleafedstrawberry|

**hour entry:** *I was entirely caught up in the testimony*

*I was entirely caught up in the testimony. There was an exit by the grandfather clock. Everyone who read the testimony put a stethoscope to every word and heard it tick. It was entirely American to be tangled up in headline wire, hanging on incident fray, the American words "grandfather clock" wired to an 1876 ballad about a clock that allegedly "after its first owner passed away, lost its sync, and after its second owner passed away, stopped ticking entirely." Children would testify to where they were in the school grounds when a lockdown started. I would testify to virtual grief. The former director of the FBI would testify to words spoken in a room, would testify to the exit by the grandfather clock, a stethoscopic metal-to-skin mid-century American coolness. The room was a kind of clock fissure and there was water pressure in the gears, the room and the instruments of our instruments exposed. We were sick of being material or trying to be material, subject to being American or trying to near subject, one or the other. We tried to enter by exiting time, by information-trying, an entirely stymying American tick.*

**second entries:** |fiddlepanic|

|fiddlepanic||silenttent||agonypoint||gingerbreadjoint|

## how many times

—after reading Orides Fontela

/how many times have you climbed
/how many times have you climbed
that hill?

/I was too close and made diagrams of the particular way
the closeness failed.

/I was too close to faith or too close to the object requiring faith
and made diagrams of the hill.
/I make a chart today a beautiful weekly chart for links and
breakages and shoulder pulls and astronaut walks /stone gears
and pigeon gurgles /AM alarms /I dropped my earring-back
in the sink /I died to the moment fox

I can't wear that I can't wear that dress Mom I wore it at Aunt X's funeral
/oatmeal is ready it's ready wake up the hill has fur theatres
in its branches /*feed someone*
*feed someone*


**hour entry:** *I was too close*

*I was too close and made diagrams of the particular way the closeness crumbled. I was too close to interrelational time seams what does it mean to be too close to faith or too close to the astronaut object requiring faith so that what you have faith in crumbles? I make a chart today a beautiful weekly chart for links and breakages and shoulder pulls and astronaut walks.*

**hour entry:** *call it rhinoceros*

*Call it grey matter in the center of the clock.*

*1:00 peripheral numbness 3:07 storm eye. I spent too long scoring symptom and symptom cost: skull pressure night-spell, screen doors shivering open shut, family exiting in and out.*

*Call it cross-beat spent wheel call it ER spoke or anchor loss call it cloudbank to the eyes, electric burn to the flower, call it anything, call it rhinoceros crabshell rash or pulse-creed thistle numbness platelet count. Looked it up on WebMD: bodies spilling taxonomies, 1:20, 7:03, petals flouncing in neural water, diagnostic blur and bleed. Medical terms as clusters of symptoms loosely held, compressed or blown like dandelion seeds. I need you to fit in the word you and be the newest body.*

## 3 vows after King Philip's perpetual prayer machine

—It is said that in the 16th century, with his son's life threatened from a head injury, King Philip II of Spain, praying, vowed to God a wondrous act in return if his son recovered—and that after his prayers were answered, he commissioned a perpetual prayer machine, an automated praying robotic monk. Such a robot is currently in the Smithsonian and attributed loosely to the king's clockmaker Juanelo Turriano. The figure makes repeated ritualistic movements such as raising a rosary, walking in a trapezoidal shape, and beating its chest in "mea culpa." It is still functional today.

1: *These two vowed they would always be together. In order to keep this vow they commissioned a dragonfly telepathy machine, two interconnected dragonfly robots that were acutely reading each other and that would connect their beings across all cities and centuries through the silence of wingbeat and prehistoric eyes. The dragonflies resembled software circuits, their bodies were pressed together with blue-black nanochip stripes and bulbs, and when they flew their wings beat with such iridescence that their entire bodies disappeared were visible only as a slight shining presence. In this way they could carry each other everywhere.*

2: *This man was hungry as a child and vowed he would never waste a cent. In order to keep this vow he had a robot built that was comprised of a tiny transformer in his ear by which each cent spent would be made to scream before being released from his hold. The scream was calculated by an algorithm assessing empty cupboards and empty cupboard fears, and the fraction of ensuing emaciation real or perceived. The scream was like no other, a combination of a fighting raccoon and an asthmatic gasp, but it would be calibrated at a mosquito pitch and played in his ear before he released each penny. In this way he learned to assess the level in any scream.*

3: *After numerous family members died unexpectedly this woman vowed not to believe in continuity at all but to believe only in the now. To keep her vow, she had a robot built that would sense expectation patterns like weather. It was comprised of an electronic weather woman who would signal safe zones and also pressure areas and patterns of permanent hope or attachment. This electronic weatherwoman was also a skilled majorette, and used her baton to point to the now-now-now of today's laughter deadline headline haircut, but whenever there was expectation forming of permanence, the weatherwoman would start twirling her batons acrobatically, quite beautifully in fact, so the two bone-like ends of it started spinning into a kind of dandelion seed blur, and from this this woman inferred alarm.*

**hour entry:** *Sorry, I am at the gym this instant*

*I am at the gym again this instant and of it, in its treadmills, its black tongues and beetle shines its oily handles in time and time and time intervals and people cupped and kept in beeps and measures, always. I'm nearly half done with my pre-programmed elliptical slot, having spent 211 calories. This very instant a woman, having come in from the street, is staring at the smeared glass of the vending machine an instant too long, the change hot in her palm, a kind of calm as yet unspent. And I am bent away from God, running horizontally in place, & all instance protests movement, all instance must be thick with protest, coated with candle wax of sadness, walking upright like unlit wicks, instance must be tricked into sequence then must read itself aflame in this.*


## this notch it's good.

/listen for the notch
/this notch in the gear it's good, it battles the snake skin,
the skin is that which is terrifying in that its coils fight.

/this one is a girl out of her uterus stems the unstilled sun,
out her mouth stems a small repeated melody.

/the clock is awake, the thumb bird is inside
being the thumb bird I heard my family patter around me,
leave for some errand half heard they will soon return I know
what the door will sound like first, then after.

**lobes of moss formed of moss**

*I'm not sure where to stand right now*
/microscopic helplessness, microscopic leaves in the leaves

>             */the moss is ribbing, islanding cement*
/certain animals appear to be standing in it
/certain people appear as nearly positioned stances
in the instrument /I refresh the browser obsessively,
watch live feeds while I walk
/today's headlines hold the world aluminum and bent
/certain creatures nestle in and in and in, certain people obsessively
tap their feet or slightly, nervously, rock

*/the moss says be in moss time, pre-language, green tick*
*/the moss says form the page in string weave, form early, form thick*
>             *but don't overly form, don't lock*

/certain creatures appear to thrive by lounging in the clock,
but barely sleep, chew on its porches of Xs, and Is, and Vs
/they wrap their torsos tight
around the iron pendulum pinecone, hook their talons
on the arrow of the hour and, head buried, slow-dance,
freeze like window cats on the minute-hand, waiting
for its soft blink of advance

**hour entry:** *Bus 15 lurched and people fell*

*Bus 15 lurched and people fell haphazardly onto people, the falling people embarrassed
to fall and call attention to themselves. See, once I shook so much speaking to a crowd,
I was falling out of speech. Once I had a watch in which the second hand was knocked
loose somehow, and shook around inside the flat glass bubble, a kind of menagerie to
loose seconds. It was a hairline faux-silver segment, a centimeter at most, and once loose,
it was not a second hand at all, but a neural-electric vein, an antenna ripped from its
insect husk, a pure uncontainment exposed by being contained.*

## crawdads being most precise

—after the differentiation between clock accuracy and clock precision,
the crawdads (with thanks to Alexis McCrossen, *Marking Modern Times*)

/crawdads being most precise, most precisely pink, in childhoods in which they were first
discovered, but never so precise again, eyelid-pink crawdads, painfully translucent pink,
so that the exoskeleton was an excuse to see the clocks within them, and when they were
exposed under rock-silt it was brutal to find them, so we wanted that brutality put our
noses close to it like the hideous wonders of deep sea fish they had no need for the armor
of skin, no need to not show their precisely wired bled organs

/no, crawdads being most personal, most like persons, in childhoods in which they were
first loved, but never children again, M. and L. and C., the crawdads should have been
painfully translucent and veined from within so that the exoskeleton was an excuse to
see the varicose network within the clockwork, so the memory of childhood friends would
always be embedded in rocks, M. would always be in plaid pants swinging in wonder
and L. would always be the castle clear girl with 5 brothers, and when they were exposed
with a stick it was a wonder to see them move and move sideways in the heart always

/crawdads being most precise when most exposed, exposed to the thought of being
excessively crawdad, my brain stem was exposed as a cauliflower or a galaxy, classrooms
were exposed by a lockdown, Americans were exposed to Americans, whole persons
were exposed in MRIs or X-rays or ultrasounds anything that shows the grey matter
of the interior clock exposed, so that the exoskeletons were an excuse to not have
exoskeletons, people subject to seeing their internal organs their loved one's organs,
unknown humans' torn organs, their twisted country's twisted organs over and over
so they had no need to not be seeking rock cover, no need to seek out anything but the
unarmored pink accuracy of awe embedded in not clocks, never clocks

/I made up some half prayer from star-veined crawdad flesh, see-through imprecision

**living within the clock means living**

/living within the clock means living
within past clocks /the golden weight
of them their little gear beaks their oily knobs

      */if you speak, speak from inhabited clusters no*
      *speak with awareness of the inhabiting clusters, but not from them*

/"meet me at the river" a gravestone reads
the apple petals fall and cover clocks the graveyard is
a weightless park that overhears all weight
      *if you speak, speak not with headlines but*
      *from unspeakable clusters of*
      *throat-tightening headlines, unspeakable counts, referents, daily*
      |speechclusters||flowerclusters||immaterialgreen|

      /I have no power to not speak

      /the last time we went to the river we did not
      go in beyond our shins
      the stones were in there for us

/the last time we went to the graveyard we had to
weed a book of grass off
to see the dates and name
      |immaterialapples|

understand me I don't love clocks
/understand me in the context
of our linear weight and in the context of the fact
we will need to leave it for the others
eventually leave the tiny weight of the flowers

**second entries:** |clippablefan|

|clippablefan||materialmoorage||aspirinforage||instancedare|
|objectsubjectswear||merelymolecular||lightlet||flagshapedbarrette|

**hour entry:** *In its free time*

*In its free time the clock tried to pretend not to be a clock. There were exquisite metallic roosters on the clock. The clock thought of roosters emerging from itself as belief sutures. The clock was naked in the locker room, naked in its notch belief. The clock used to believe it held the locker room clock-numb, everyone in their instruments of their instruments. There was an awkward sense of praying in the feather semblance, praying in the bathroom breaks, praying in the moment beaks. I was so close to my family I couldn't see them merely in time. The clock believed it was getting closer and closer it had to be unbearably close to the runners' cleats to the padlock click to hear itself.*

## the uncertainty principle in the pulse

/pulsatile tinnitus so that the attention is drawn from the rainclouds
to the interior raincloud
/the uncertainty principle in the pulse /did the heart race did it not?

*I have the feeling I have partially stopped and the others have sped up*
*on the way to the orchard*
/to be too close to the blood
to be so close to the blood so that you are far away from the peachtree
and the raincloud

/the uncertainty in medical imaging
/the raincloud of the jugular vein in excessive proximity to the inner
pieces of the ear
the unfounded fear I will not wake up and will not be able to express the beauty
of the raincloud
I heard my blood all day /the instruments of monitor express
continuity or distress /the distance from here to the raincloud
/demographic rates and peaks,
symptoms leaking semblances of ancestral symptoms
*I am uncertain as to the color of my own cheeks*
/excessive proximity so that attention is drawn away
/the blood pressure monitor, gym elliptical, manual hill setting, EKG

how many heartbeats in such fear /how many heartbeats
from here to the principle of certainty? /did your raincloud emit peaches?

*/gloriously sunset-colored peaches unlike anything yellow*
/if one clock stops, the other clocks continue though they are
synced through peach trunks

*the fear that I was distracted*
*by measuring stops and starts and missed out on reaching the actual*
*orchard overflow of peaches, I smelled their ever-dust*
/the measures of measure exhausted us

**second entries:** |caterpillarpillar|

|caterpillarpillar||extremesteam||disbeliefin||pushpinhope||thindoorsplint|

**hour entry:** *The animal was a light fixture*

*I was privileged to have time to write this on a weekend with gauze curtains and electric light before my eyes. I was privileged to be fed and for the most part unscathed and able to follow the animals of my fingertips moving in purchased light.*

*The animal was a light fixture, no the animal was the industry of pocketwatches and light fixtures, the animal was the industry and the privilege was an economic privilege to hold the control of light or time in the animal. It had a mechanical heart, yes, the animal had a mechanical heart and it was more dependable than any palpitation it cut through. There were people who worked in factories to create mechanical clocks or unburnt fuses, their tiny spindle valves from dawn to dusk, that was the workday, dawn to dusk. They were soft, softer than boiled beet flesh, softer than oyster pulp, softer than luck. The animal crawled into them and they crawled into the animal.*

**second entries:** |lickedthreadfray|

|lickedthreadfray||beginningsstay||demographicflowerclusters|
|wreathspeech||spelloutpercent||pluckedtent||sickdayflint|

## what coils then fall out of the sun?

*And if the cuckoo clock measured sundials?*
*If the sundials measured governments measured instruments*
*measured waterwheels?*
*If you had to say what this tenth of a second feels like?*

I'd be leaning forward, forward
out of it sliver, out of its hold, out of its marigold,
out of its nuclear leak, its sunset, its name,
out of the off-kilter minute, excruciating exacted minutes occur,
out of the tv-news helicopter, its blade whir,
jaw fit, out of the caught tilt of the waterwheel,
the wheeling want of it…

*What coils then fall out of the sun?*
*What industries fall out of yourself?*

what balance spring /reflecting quadrant /chronometer /chain factory /monk
prayer /solar time /anchor escapement /verge and balance /dragon fixture /paper
dragon /bearded serpent /wheel arm /doctor watch /stop watch /vertical spoke
/arm dial /escape wheel metal tongue /So Sung water clock /mammoth skull
/imperial symbol /civil war pocket watch /reflecting quadrant /anchor scale
/quartz clock /quartz watch /clepsydra /alleged flow alleged siren glow /alleged
ambulance rooster dragon /A theory /B theory /Harrison's sea watch /astrolabe
/wretched bird /cuckoo bird /knight in armor /elusive inventor of the anchor
escapement /sundial /pilot watch /satellite mainspring /dragon tooth water rate
/late late late rescue /oscillation navigation /elusive inventor of the cave-dwelling
/Galileo's pendulum /electric skin atomic bells /railroad shudder /firework tube
/factory time /fail quadrant /chime and chime and chime and chime

**hour entry:** *Orchids because orchids are impossibly mimicking*

*Orchids because orchids are impossibly mimicking the milk fluid capture of being orchids, orchids because they are grown commercially in soldiering rows in hothouse tents, because they are given as gifts for merely being orchids, because they are inherently exceeding themselves and held as if rare, though they are not, their stems are second hands untimed and slightly skewed so binding. Orchids because they are wrist-colored, because they are eyelid textured, because they are partial light captured, because they are hard to keep living. And on the slope of a hillside of a rainforest of my childhood was an orchid nursery. I don't know I ever entered it, but knew the plastic walls sweat.*

## the birth of chronology

/the birth of chronology a crisis in which horizontal lines must flow
|applecorebruise||whosecreation|
blanket-bound, the universe sang

/post Big Bang, we want to unlock before
          |beforebruisedfruit||beforenation|

/I have to continue with my day despite the reported day I want to enter
prayer without entering time for prayer
/the crisis of America's last mass shooting in which
the report tries to unlock before

/the Big Bang a sarcastic term spoken by the physicist
who didn't agree with it, before it took hold

          /one wants to unlock multiverse or stratospheres I want to unlock
          the turning fruit

/you cannot look at intention alone that is the error, you
cannot look at nasturtium wilt alone that is
/you cannot look all the reports simultaneously that is the
error |applelook||profileappearance||nextpagenextapple|
*I wanted to stay curled in the blanket like before*

/before we were precise the chronology included precise fiction |slipsatin|
|bodyblanketlook||Americanexposure| the cinematic
shutting of the dead woman's eyelids over and over
/the birth of fiction in the chronology

          /the choice of can't continue must continue
*I am here in the blanket, creation*

*I am tuning my ears I am reestablishing my ears*
|harkenapple||darkpanic|
/torque and gear physics reportedly expired, the report exhausted of reporting

/to unhinge narrative so as to prevent future narrative
the birth of nonchronology |purelight||applewhite||safetynetstarlitneteverlit|
so let it, let us live extremely
even from a blanket

**hour entry:** *If I feel my limbs in the orangewood*

*I feel I have done an injustice by saying we are in the cuckoo clock at all. I say I in you and I in we while the polka dancers are many. They are stolid solid wooden rotations and we are in a rotation but I am not you. You may not have wanted to enter that melody you may have been barred from it by its aprons and hands. People are called they or we and I say they for the nation then we then decide on a dragon's jaw splitting orange wood in half leaking new sun. The polka dancers cannot feel their limbs; they simply enter and spin from some disparate moment into the half hour cuckoo chime. I speak to myself as an orbit and then I speak to you as a waterwheel. I feel you are your own orbit convening somewhere in this apparatus where I am trying to speak.*

**second entries:** |menageriestare|

|menageriestare||airandpurchase||furnaceinstant||notidentity|
|moonaffinity||nottoohot||soot'shot||howmanyfit||owlethole|

## 4 minutes in the vertical garden

—after choreography curation notes from a collaborative performance involving
movement through three stations (an object shrine, an open locker cubby hole and a
vertical garden) prompted by alarms

/welcome soon snooze-button 10-minute dream-sets soon
|axisfight||zinniagears| and |stemmingday|

/welcome /you have 4 minutes in the unsteady sway
of the vertical garden /you can take leaf moss from your roof
/chicken wire is required,
secrecy and scarcity, tiredness is required

*/I feel strongly it should not be downstairs*
/you can take godspeed no one will see it directly
/you can take yourself to it, it will be
housed in the globe shelter /the clock can hang from it with twine

/soon you will be in the vertical garden
/welcome /wake /rotate zinnia gears and wake
/you can put the ball of your foot vertically against the test clover,
but not your weight, the late trajectory lesson will cost you
/how do you coalesce and move
|snapdragondewspit||newsfeeddrill||knicknacksale|
/show me how to tantrum trip
/show me how to lockdown play

welcome you have /1 minute in which your spirit roofless lives
/a walkway of light

/no a slit that makes a walkway /you can fit
your alarm states leaking missiles neural corpuscles somehow neatly in
/welcome chlorophyll drift, emotional pore, freight
*I feel I should wait here in the leaf until it's not mere interval*
|slipperscuff||whitezinniabentstiff|

/intervals between shopping malls /intervals between
apple slices /freeway crises /drone dice /intervals between latest types of
bloodshed /welcome /the digital gone haywire
and people having 10-minute sleepsets

/show me how to vinecurl pixel sieve
/show me how to leave the slit
of God open safe and green in the leaf ruin
/the flitting horizontal was not the destination anyway /welcome
|flowerballs||spinclusters||griefgraffiti||sleepingraccoons|

welcome /laboratory hands are required /flimsy metallic houses
are required /the tension in music box knobs is required,
tangled wires, governments splayed and split
/soon, any movement forward prayerless can feel brutal
/I feel if you look down you could fall off the staircase
/how do you disrupt forward kilter
|zinniameter ||gunfilter|
/how do you place the axis
of your spine in the seizure of alarm

/welcome you have 2 minutes in which to lift yourself vertical
/chickenwire will keep your ever life from spilling
/how do you arachnid-pray
how do you arrow-flow

/you have 3 minutes welcome you have 3 minutes to say
good morning to your child
|insertheadkiss||smallforeheadthis|

/the digital gone haywire and people sheltered in mere interval
/doled out horizontal 10-minute dreamsets, a snooze-button oracle asking
/if your head is a pendulum

/if upon exiting the clock the belovedness of everyone becomes integral
/if the leaves are as wide as your shoulder-blades, you are complete here
/if your legs have become small and the apple has become gargantuan
/if the disaster has become small and the clover has failed you

|flowerballs||zinniaclustersspeechclusters||inhabitancememe|
I feel I should lie horizontally and settle my feet vertically in the clover
/how do you laboratory-click,
resync armed seed, American ground-spout
/show me to trip automatic violence out

/and what will you say to your love?
what did you say to the child?

/if everyone in fact every finger hooking itself on the chickenwire of prayer
disorienting clocks is welcome
*/I feel I have 4 minutes to grow into a vine*

*/I feel the leaves coalesce and climb, or*
*/it is still just morning, and my family is just fine*
                                                    /show me how to sieve or move
                                            how do you lava-flow rope-chord
                                    how do you instance-horde innocence-stow

/if all your waiting arteries were still arterial
pre-alarm |blueblazer||redcurl| if you hunt and unfurl in the clock
*/where are you and where are they?*

              */it is 7:39 and your bow drops*
                  it is 7:39 and where is your head and your heart?
/imperfections in the floor you would only see if your head
was rocking to your pulse, 10 seconds spilled from ever then

|insertinertia||flipperpetal||windstillthen||wind&wind|

**hour entry:** *I would speak*

*I would speak something invisibly like a marigold and it would disappear in the space in*
*which God forgives clock-sense, and offers up the leaves of the marigolds as sentries.*

## song to jump rope inside the clock

—after "Sterling & Noble," a table clock brand

sterling and noble
wooden and feeble
fox-like and nimble
golden and labeled

sterling and sterling and sterling and sterling and
itch like a second hand, watch like a fox
1-2-3-4-5 *(keep going until you trip)*

sterling and feeble
prisoned and labeled
rock-like and able
golden and liable

prisoned unprisoned unprisoned and prisoned and
notch like a second hand, click like a rock
1-2-3-4-5-6 *(keep going until you trip)*

sterling and global
wooden and fabled
fox-like and feeble
golden and nimble

golden and golden and golden and golden and
catch like a second hand, count like a flock
1-2-3-4-5-6-7 *(keep going)*

## now accumulate

/even now, the whole snow
/even now, to want for you the whole snow
/to want for you the whole unspeakable forecasted breath-hold
/and clocklessness of snow, from beginning to beginning
/the entire ragged cloud inversion act of snow
/the whole socked in oxygenated purity of possible snow
/the whole opal evanescent wall from which the smallest mentionable
/whole white flick of snow scatters not even down
/scatters, sideways, up, like some mistake to the eye
/and ultimately locates gravity, falls, and someone calls
/*It's snowing*, or says *Snowflakes* or *Mom look! Snow!*
/even post miscalculation, pre-rupture pre-engine stall
/post roll-call, pre-wall pre-legislative suture even now
/early century, even now post ice-sting pre-sung terror
/to want for you the incalculable collection of lacework intricacy
/the most miniscule crochet shape of the snowflake
/the smallest whole possible snowflake
/its molecular-knit possibility, the whole individuation
/of the uncalculated snowflake falling on the now and the now
/and the now, how it is merely enough to call itself itself
/among accumulates of minutes and cloud-held clock-ticks
/pre-now, reforming steeples of now
/accumulates of too late hate-disruption tricks
/and accumulates called a nation and accumulates
/of hopelessness stationed mid-soiled cloud
/among spun-out tire paralysis and spray
/among accumulate of wealth lust and forecast distrust
/among the whole dirty accumulate of speech
/and aspersion and slush among whole unspoken
/half-inch caterpillar puffs of snow accumulation
/among whole protests and whole abominations
/sticking, to want for you to want for you, at least
/the incalculable particulate of softness in people
/the fierce icy softness of people sticking together
/people in protest sticking together /by the least of
their temporal edges, a molecular softness shifting slow
/holding each other steady by their elbows

## I walked through handwritten clouds

"All clocks are clouds." —Michael Palmer

/there was no one
on the playground maybe swingset dew

/I was leaning toward belief that I can speak
with you a while while speech
leaks out of us in failed flower clusters

/italic numerals mechanically pinned
to the clockface the clockface to the sun

/I walked through over-said worlds, I walked
through handwritten clouds

/the aspiration *"I am always*
*praying"* are you always praying

/the pressurized cloud bank: always


**hour entry:** *I fall asleep with a rain sound*

*I fall asleep with the rain sound app of my cellphone, the app includes distant thunder clap sounds and there are people who recorded or simulated these sounds, and it is time to disagree and thank the dawn. I disagree with this rain, I feel absurd for the simulation of it and yet my brain waves have come to depend on it, depend on simulated porous points between the raindrops. Always the porous dream, always the neural authority, the reaction meme, always the authority of always, the puncture of always, time spent saying always, the spider legs of always, the sleep command, the wake spindles, the spider leg threatening to break from the spider.*

## more a clothespin

/the cuckoo more a plug in time, a jab, proclaiming itself at half-hour intervals

/more a clothespin than a bird, a notch of wood dipped
in yellow yelling melodic chime
/more a punctuating clothespin, more insertion and emotion

/more a temporal jabbing voting season, proclamation, claiming
midweek love or fiscal haunt or sunrise leak
and seeing the gears through every and each alarm

/more a cuckoo than a thought, more a tree line than a gear

/more an approximation of myself, pronoun-making, minute-staking
/more a filament of the melodic cuckoo-ticking earth

/here the ever-clock of clothespins /chime of when
we were unbranched neural electric fear, when we were perched
like birds on a Monterey pier, chime of our own blood astir

/over and over, approximate nearness crying, local sirens and chimes,
heat stains from the iron drying
/oh clock o'clock oh children of clothespins

/when they were 5 they would run to the cuckoo chime
whatever they were doing, scramble up the couch to see its yellow notch emerge

/more the song and unsung minutes /more when and when
so porous it hurts

/more cost of porousness /the scent of loss in certain T-shirts

/more I am the cuckoo bird puncture claiming two notes only I or we
true or here 5-year or forever escapement or gear

/back to the impossible filament of self we thought we were rid of it but
then the alarm the alarm the daily lever and who
wakes beside whose ears here in this Tuesday far from never

**hour entry:** *Can the clock burn*

*Can the clock burn? Why can't the clock burn? It is accustomed to flame anyway it is the tooth of the flame anyway. Why can't a tooth burn? It does not burn because even if it burns it is embodied in affective rotations, nasturtiums prayer-wilt anyway, people live so close to all they may lose any second anyway. But can the clock burn? This is not about a clock at all but what the clock surrounds, the clock as a moat, the clock as a moat of charred clock parts, arbors, pivots, pinions, escape wheels, I'm talking about the instruments of promises and satellites and deadlines and rants and all one circles talking to oneself, sensing burn, I'm talking about the measure around the unmeasured, the center of the nebula that fails to hold or holds excessively. The clock surrounds a fiery center, a foliage of flame, clockless. It's Sunday and I'm writing my heart out to get free of the clock, it's the noonish center of Sunday and P. is knocking around the kitchen beside me.*

**minute ballad**

If I was Taylor's bricklayer
if I was so efficient,
I'd reduce myself by 7 years
and shave off extra movement.

**I have been over-concerned with touchpoint.**

/*I have been over-concerned with touchpoint, oh clock. I have been hovering over
a pond of glazed clay and lips and tipping rocks and speech cluster fits.*

/over touch, i.e. the touch can be grasped so hard that the glass
of the surface disappears.
/over touch, i.e. it can be so soft that it defines itself in a spectral awareness that
only like touch perceives, so is invisible to much of the touching world.

/of course, there was actual intimate touch wherein the body is turned
into a pond shape with the knowledge from the interior depths
that the exterior depths shimmer and the interiority of this pond shape
mixes and remakes.

/over-closeness an ache, so that, I am where?
/*of course there is the flitter of next /of course there is the calligraphed pond.*

/there is an error in the repetition of the clock, it is the error
of the obsessive green weave interrupting
the pond surface and making it, it is the error
of the incantation of time reading backward and forward simultaneously
so becoming in itself a living medium.

/*I have been overly zip, touching pendulum dip, instrument scare.*
/*I have been expanding water lip.*
/*I lifted the coffee cup. I put down the pen.*
/in every action, the desire to be closer to the action an impatience culminating
into immaterial crux or shine
too much to carry into the next pond-shimmer and so I am, where?

/*I hold a cup made by my son with black dots painted around the rim intended to
represent blackberries.*

**second entries:** |nojokingill|

|nojokingill||neuraloverfill||whippoorwillover|
|gillflapdoor||*don'tsaynever*||hisslightfever|

**hour entry:** *horizontal walkers*

*What is the digital clock afraid of? Horizontal walkers. What is the locker room afraid of? Vertical gardens. What is the clock afraid of? Horizon after horizon becoming the same horizon. What are the living afraid of? Nuclear pink. What are the dead afraid of? Not clocks. What are the clocks afraid of? Everything the dead forgot. What do nights say about sunsets? All pinkness looks the same.*

*Everyone loved the terminology of the clock even more than the clock, they loved the allure of the object, the escapement the free-wheel the strike, and talked as if they were petition merely as if they were apart from the horology they petitioned. I am afraid for people being overly mechanical about heart-and-flesh people the same way I am afraid for people not being literal about overreliance on the notch, and I rely on such fear to pray.*

**minute ballad**

Announcing Pendulum Freeze:
half the instrument in grief,
half the instrument ceased
to recognize grief and move.

**if I open up the clock,**

/what I meant to measure clunks down the stairs like language, falls
/all clocks, instruments, all instruments, cares

/instrument after instrument in the tightness of timed air /excessive
instrumentation, new kitchenware, cell phone welcomes, instruments
of excess and excess causing scarcity causing fear /42% here home with guns
/ripping instruments, mundane instruments, melodic instrument too

/the instrument of ribbon clusters falling off
birthday gifts, and people lifting wheelchairs, and the trying strain of prayer
/the clumsy standing and kneeling of the congregation,
squeaks of wood /someone's mother making dinner,
the reuse of the strainer /unspool instrument /unspool spool

/I am too close to speech clusters too close
to clunking tools, heard frailties, falls /at the end of my measure,
at the directional end,
at the constellated unfelt orbiting night of *there is no clock at all*

*orbiting light merely, orbiting dream*

/to pray by merely moving, move with antelopes I've never seen,
their blessed whisk legs running

**hour entry:** *the act of saying "orchid"*

*I held an artificial orchid, felt a second hand arrow as a thin orchid stem. One side of the orchid is pointing at everything close, one side of time is not accepting timelessness, its obliteration stain. A friend writes on Facebook of the species of flowers: "if you love something learn its name" and people are sloppy with the actual belovedness of the arrow, the loose galaxy-hold "I love" is not the same as the holding of the arrow by the clock. I held an artificial orchid and the act of saying "orchid" brings the silkenness of its made presence in held time, near. I mean the orchid-fury of naming, this side of here.*

**hour entry:** *The hawk is an approximate whisking together*

*The hawk is an approximate whisking together of fractions of itself the 23 intervals
in the second the eye can see the 500 intervals in the second the ear can hear the 100
intervals in the second the bird can see. The second is forming midair like any duration
or station in sun. Say "look a red-tailed hawk" and in that second the alliterative span
of flashes of light formed by a moving pinking-sheared wing shape becomes it. I wish my
words to become unfit for a second, to not make such blurred sad sounds. The unspoken
fractions of our seconds are expressed imprecisely all the time in seconds. "I'll be there in
a second." "He was gone in a second." "The next second they were on the ground."*

**minute ballad**

Over once upon a once-hood
and thrice upon a second
over 6 million girlhoods,
the eternal coelacanth.

## 20 s. elegy

—after reports of a private plane hitting a vacation house, the family in the house having 20 seconds to react

/20 seconds to retrieve to collect 20 seconds
/go straight for the thing you intended to lift and lift
/we saw an eagle through a lens looking straight at the lens
/which was the best intention I lost it remembered the eagle
/at the end of twenty seconds the interval of eagles
/I said to 20 s. I believe in the child and the eagle
/the mussel black darkness in which we slipped
/rehearsed or not we grab something before us
/the one with the impulse lived the one with the run-through impulse
/it started at 11 and ended at 3, the 20 seconds
/it started at the sun and ended at the sun
/go straight for the thing you intended to lift and lift
/lift the sea to the eyes of the child the eyes of the child to the sea
/which was the best intention I lost it remembered the eagle
/start at the 6 and end at the 10 but not numbers
/the mussel black darkness protected mussels thick
/it starts at the waking and ends at the variation of waking
/go straight for the thing you intended to lift and lift
/the closest I got was lifting the child to the eagle
/lift the sea to the eyes of the child the eyes of the child to the sea
/at the end of 20 s. the interval of eagles
/go straight for the thing you intended to lift and lift
/which was the best intention I lost it remembered the eagle
/the 20 s. at the end of which inheritance blooms
/grab something to leave for the others grab eagles
/the one with the run-through impulse, light through a lens
/the eagle looked straight at the child and the child at the eagle
/time enough to forget who you are and run corners
/go straight for the thing you intended to lift and lift
/which was the best intention I lost it remembered the eagle
/it began at the 5 and ended at 9 and was over
/if you cut between the eagle and the sea how many divisions?
/which was the best intention I lost it remembered the child
/skip what I said before about beginning and ending
/I refuse to think it ends where the 20th second ends
/I refuse to think it starts with numerals again
/skip the part about eagles and go to the child
/skip the part about 20 and go to the black of the mussel

**hour entry:** *It was like I was the cuckoo clock's mother.*

It was like I was the cuckoo clock's mother. There were transparent frogs and plastic horses and the clarity of children on earth. I saw through one wrist to another. There was another plastic horse it was purchased it was in a family of duplicate horses. Different children loved duplicate horses differently, so braided their manes similarly.

There was another clock in another room buzzing.

**The clock failed to measure worlds before the clock.**

/before was made of incorrect calculations of the correct orchid /no before was
made of correct calculations of incorrect waters /after was made of impenetrable
stillness against which a potted orchid moves /I am free to destroy the clock,
I am free to forget it and fall into orchid milk sleep /before the clock ticked, we
calculated it was about to tick /Facebook calculates the number of friends and
calculates anniversaries of virtual friendship /I depend on friends but at times
hesitate to call friends friends /people step into the rumor of certain callings and
certain war /people step into certain structures on which they depend because
they have nowhere else to step /I depend on being able to ruffle my son's hair on
occasion /the sun depends on nitrogen goblins /I am free to believe or not in the
miracle of Cairo's Mary apparition and the uncalculated encompasses my belief
/nothing is calculated in the alleged nitrogen of the sun /the universe depends
on ferns /new wars depend on previous wars /before I am fully awake I depend
on curtain-sifted light /before the election there was a firmness to shivering ferns,
and after /I am free to fill the silence with denser silence /I am free to destroy
the lineage of horological failures /we had 3 days of ice, then more /a friend
miscalculated the ice and slipped and broke her jaw /there is no law to calculation
of love /at the end there will be a certain orchid silence akin to prayer /there will
be a certain air akin to fractured ice

**second entries:** |verticalsieve|

|verticalsieve||empiricalstir||shewasfallingandIcaughther|
|milkshakemiracle||Newtonianizedparticle||falteringoflimbs||cloudsim|

**hour entry:** *perfect perfect*

*The veins in the leaf were perfect perfect. The veins in the leaf were perfectly consecutive, tiny ribs, fluted with water, so all clocks were flattered by the presence of all leaves and loved them. I meant to be able to spill out whole leaf sense when needed for those I loved, I meant to be able to do more than bring in from the garden a single handful of basil leaf. The wholeness of people is unfathomable it is terrified of itself.*

*I meant to be able to spill leaflessness into chlorophyll, to be daily green and not simultaneously |saintpointillist||diffusedfist||todolistsquill|. Whole people will shoot whole people today like yesterday somewhere. Whole people will turn themselves inside out for love. Their eyelids have slight ribbing veins like the leaves.*

**minute ballad**

Announcement from the marsh: a forum
for Parmenides and disciples,
if there is no passage of time,
all dragonflies are syllables.

81

**hour entry:** *I felt I had not done justice*

"We shall see that we have a constant feeling sui generis of pastness, to which every one of our experiences in turn falls a prey." —William James

*I felt I had not done justice to the exaction of experience as leaf flit, so the exaction retreated.*

*I used to think the world of this child making this clay girl this leaf-guy snake or crumble or cry was the most accurate fiction. I used to think I could enter cloud continuance. I used to think that the transactional world where people fought to not whither in false transaction was the actual action. Then I thought that the interior implausible symmetry of the astrolabe was the implicit revolution. I used to think the injustice of instrumentation was the most tragic marigold. Then I thought that the world of the historical accumulation of prayer was the actual fairytale. Then that it was not about entrance at all, it was not about fairytale at all, it was about leaking or exiting out of the measure, out of the second, about the inability for the second to hold the pressure of the policy of the dewdrop. I once thought that simultaneous rainbows in three parts of the earth and simultaneous violence in one nation was the most unspeakable simultaneity. I thought all speech unhinged from its referent, the clock unhinged from that which it measured, the runner unhinged from the race, but chasing it, so the clock was a kind of love sicknesses toward time's unmeasured milk swirls and jewels of light cake shivering.*

**hour entry:** *drench delay*

*After it had not rained at all all August, after the ash fall dulled even the smallest oily leaves and we breathed forest fire threat and sweat and slowness, on September 29, at 5:17 it down-poured briefly vertically like a scolding of relief and joy and even after the downpour, the sky vault empty, the leaves, not the sky at 6:03 kept raining, the leaves had caught rain in their rips and wilts and spines and spores, the oaks, salal and blackberry vines, they made a secondary rain sound identical to sky-drop but more gifted, it was this leaf-held dialectic train of rain this drench delay I hope to name sometime, in future heat, for you.*

**minute ballad**

The soot came through the kitchen vent
the fumes came through the door,
the forest fire wore a long skirt
although the fire was over.

## I am not a visitor

/I would like to feel I am not a visitor, I am
        not a visitor to digital time, fictional and lit
/I am not a marigold in the vertical garden,
        I am not a visitor in the orbit
/a fox was lying finite in it, everyone I knew raced and raced
        every Saturday even, everyone
/even love was too close to language too far
        from nursery rhyme in marigold gold
/the holding of time was maternal was infernal
        was hot with sunset and petal
/I heard the marigold burning sipping sun
        continue sipping sun
/I heard my own love run immeasurably close
        a silken sense of arteries effacing ticks
/the fox was never to be predicted, I couldn't find evidence of it
        never being an actual fox
/a song as menace to expanse eats the unbeknownst,
        darts in and out, snatches chickens
/everyone almost everyone
        had a laptop propped up at the coffee shop
/everyone was racing even clocks raced other clocks
        but it was a race to meet, to sync
/once upon a once upon a once upon a once upon
        a once becomes a kind of illness of once-hood
/the marigolds once had awkwardly stiff stems
        shooting upward, so were vulnerable to break
/I would like to feel I am not a visitor I am not
        a visitor to the second notch of the marigold
/I would like to feel I am praying always, so never
        must be in prayer too, automatic weapons too
/I caught myself in horizontal quilts drawing out
        pale curlicues of thread
/once upon a time a nursery rhyme was God's fever
        God held a hand to God's forehead and snowed
/everyone was racing snatching each other out
        of the snow out of the office out of the TV crime show
/to snatch actual eyelashes loved while praying, snatch actual days
        without mention of days
/today's pronouncement: to hold time must be free
        of the word "once," free of the pounce of it

/no not snow not snow no not mere incident of
                        softness, no not twice in two days no
/only snow will stop the sound of traffic only
                        warning shots shoot upward into nothing
/to hold any swaddled infant in the middle
                        of time bursting out of her swaddle
/I believe the fox is a kind of animal flower
                        given to measure to mock it
/I believe I have never seen a fox but my son
                        saw two in the suburbs at night, two
/the runners race horizontally round and round
                        the high school track but not without vertical ache
/I am not a visitor to the field I am not a visitor
                        to the asteroid-gifted snow in the orbit of the field
/the thing about bullets they seldom shoot up,
                        the thing about nursery rhymes they never get old
/vertical worlds fall horizontally, that is the sadness,
                        that is the awful green sadness of the marigolds

**second entries:** |counterscounthem|

|counterscounthem||seventyone||slipsoftongue||avenuesIsung|
        |intoavenues||sevenlatches||intocavernous||timesnatches|
|climbboulder||higherhigher||sixslipwire||counttheireyes||eightsuns|

## Acknowledgements

Thank you to the editors of the following publications in which poems from this book, some in earlier versions, first appeared:

*Bennington Review*

*Burnside Review*

*Denver Quarterly*

*February, an anthology*

*13 Hats at Mothers Foucault's*

*Interim*

*Make It True, Poetry from Cascadia*

*New American Writing*

*Ostrich Review*

*periodicities*

*VOLT*

*West Branch*

Warm thanks to Omnidawn Publishing, especially to my wonderful editor and publisher Rusty Morrison for her clarity and close attention which helped me to see this manuscript to its final form. Worlds of thanks to executive director Laura Joakimson for her care and expertise with this book at every point in the publishing and design process. Grateful acknowledgment to the late Ken Keegan, and gratitude to all at Omnidawn for their vision and their kindness.

Thanks to the artists and writers of the former 13 Hats collaborative (2011-13) in Portland, Oregon, where the first seeds of this manuscript began, specifically as an entry for the "banker's box" collaboration. Thank you to the organizers of the Pure Surface reading series, and to Dawn Stoppiello and Ajna Lichau for collaborating in a 2015 performance through that series. Thank you to the PLAYA residency program for artists, writers, and natural scientists, for granting me a residency in summer 2016 in Summer Lake, Oregon, where I worked on this project.

Thank you to Mary Szybist for her kindness and astute attention in reading and responding to innumerable versions. Love and gratitude to my husband Patrick Playter Hartigan for helping me to see closely into this work at every stage, among all else. I am grateful to everyone who read, heard or discussed this project in its many iterations, who helped me dwell in this work and see it forward, including Sam Lohmann, Jen Coleman, Anna Daedalus, Lisa Fink, Phoebe Wayne, Allison Cobb, Eliza Rotterman, Michele Glazer, Dan Beachy-Quick, and numerous others. Thank you always to my loving parents and family. Many thanks to the authors cited for introducing me to some of the history of clocks and time measure and other information which played into my imagining.

Thanks with all my heart to Patrick and our son Jackson for their love and support, an underpinning to all my time.

# Notes

epigraph—"Letter in April: IV" (three-line excerpt) by Inger Christensen, translated by Susanna Nied, from LIGHT, GRASS, & LETTER IN APRIL, copyright ©1979 by Inger Christensen. Translation copyright © 2011 by Susanna Nied. Reprinted by permission of New Directions Publishing Corp.

I'm talking about their rotation—information in the epigraph on the nilometer: Robert Levine, Chapter 3, "A Brief History of Clock Time" in *A Geography of Time: The Temporal Misadventures of a Social Psychologist, or How Every Culture Keeps Time Just a Little Bit Differently* (New York: Basic Books, 1997), 61. "Nilometer," Wikipedia, Wikipedia Foundation, en.wikipedia.org/wiki/Nilometer. Text is available under the Creative Commons Attribution-ShareAlike License 3.0. The Wikipedia information is attributed to Helaine Selin, Editor, *Encyclopaedia of the History of Science, Technology, and Medicine in Non-Western Cultures* (Boston: Dordrecht, 1997) and to Brian Fagan, *The Great Warming: Climate Change and the Rise and Fall of Civilizations* (New York: Bloomsbury Press, 2008).

hour entry: *All bells must hold all clocks*—clocca is from the Oxford English Dictionary entry on clock, etymology, med. Latin.

hour entry: *When John Adams wrote*—"clocks were a tolling of public events" draws information from Alexis McCrossen, "Time's Tongue and Hands: The First Public Clocks in the U.S." in *Marking Modern Times: A History of Clocks, Watches, and other Timekeepers in American Life* (Chicago: The University of Chicago Press, 2013), 24-31. The line "Thirteen Clocks were made to Strike together" is quoted in McCrossen, *Marking Modern Times*, 31-32, and the originally public domain source is from: John Adams, letter "From John Adams to Hezekiah Niles on the American Revolution 13 February 1818," Archives, founders.archives.gov/documents/Adams/99-02-02-6854. [This is an Early Access document from *The Adams Papers*, founders.archives.gov/about/Adams. It is not an authoritative final version.]

hour entry: *Here is a school bus moving through the pink dawn*—information on daylight savings time: Carlene E. Stephens, *On Time: How America Has Learned to Live by the Clock* (Boston, New York, London: Smithsonian Institution, 2002), 122.

the longest hour is the shortest—written in memory of the 2015 mass shooting at Umpqua Community College, Roseburg, Oregon.

the cuckoo before it emerges—after a reading by Mary Jo Bang, Reed College, 2015.

23 clocks and instruments of removal—the original version of this poem accompanied a photo diary of the clocks in my life on a given workday, written as part of the collaborative box project, specifically the banker's box, with the artist-writer collaborative group 13 Hats. The box was displayed in the gallery show 13 Hats at 12×16 in 2013.

hour entry: *In Milwaukie, in 1908*—information on the Milwaukie incident is summarized from: McCrossen, *Marking Modern Times*, 128-30.

hour entry: *It is reported*—information on the incense clock: Levine, *A Geography of Time*, 56. Silvio A Bedini. "The Scent of Time. A Study of the Use of Fire and Incense for Time

Measurement in Oriental Countries," Transactions of the American Philosophical Society, 53, no. 5 (1963): 1–51. www.jstor.org/stable/1005923.

**hour entry:** *This noon*—information on time zones: Stephens, *On Time*, 102-103.

**my superhero is made of crunched up chandeliers**—for Jackson.

**hour entry:** *Start the stopwatch. The animal was a light fixture, no the animal was a shovel*—information on Frederick Winslow Taylor: Adam Frank, *About Time: Cosmology and Culture at the Twilight of the Big Bang* (New York: Free Press, a Division of Simon & Schuster, Inc., 2011), 322-323. Stephens, *On Time*, 167-169.

**hour entry:** *That it never*—information in the epigraph: Liz Evers, *It's About Time: From Calendars and Clocks to Moon Cycles and Light Years - A History* (London: Michael O'Mara Books Limited, 2013), 103. Carolus Linnaeus, *Linnaeus' Philosophia Botanica* (Oxford: Oxford University Press, 2005), 295. Accessed April, 2022. ProQuest Ebook Central.

**hour entry:** *I was entirely caught up in the testimony*—the Oxford English Dictionary attributes the source of the term grandfather clock to the title of a song by H.C. Work, 1876, "My Grandfather's Clock." The phrase "after its first… ticking entirely" is a variation from a sentence on the song at: Grandfather Clock, Wikipedia, Wikipedia Foundation, en.wikipedia.org/wiki/Grandfather_clock. Text is available under the Creative Commons Attribution-ShareAlike License 3.0. The Wikipedia information is attributed to: grandfather-clock-info.com. The lines "The former director of the FBI… by the grandfather clock…" reference: James B. Comey, Senate Select Committee on Intelligence, Statement for the Record, June 8, 2017, www.intelligence.senate.gov/sites/default/files/documents/os-jcomey-060817.pdf.

**how many times**—after reading Orides Fontela, *Collected Poems*, 1966-1996, (Berkeley: Neo-baroque/Grand Quiskadee, 2011).

**3 vows after King Philip's perpetual prayer machine**—information in the epigraph: Evers, *It's About Time*, 87. Description of "Automaton of a Friar," Smithsonian National Museum of American History, Behring Center, americanhistory.si.edu/collections/search/object/nmah_855351%E2%80%9D. Elizabeth King, "Clockwork Prayer, a 16th century mechanical monk," *Blackbird*, Vol 1, No 1 (2002), blackbird.vcu.edu/v1n1/nonfiction/king_e/prayer_introduction.htm.

**crawdads being most precise**—information in the epigraph on the differentiation between accuracy and precision: McCrossen, *Marking Modern Times*, 11.

**living within the clock means living**—after a visit to Sun Rise cemetery, Wasco, Oregon, "meet me at the river" remembered from a gravestone there.

**what coils then fall out of the sun?**—after reading Jimena Canales, *A Tenth of a Second, A History* (Chicago: The University of Chicago Press, 2009).

**the birth of chronology**—information on the term Big Bang: Frank, *About Time*, 202-203.

**4 minutes in the vertical garden**—draws from dance curation notes, planning, and the experience of a collaborative performance through the Pure Surface series in Portland,

Oregon with dancer Dawn Stoppiello and artist Ajna Lichau in 2015.

**now accumulate**—with thanks to poet Allison Cobb for her words "we are all particles" after the 2016 election.

**I walked through handwritten clouds**—epigraph from "Autobiography" by Michael Palmer, from *AT PASSAGES*, copyright ©1995 by Michael Palmer. Reprinted by permission of New Directions Publishing Corp.

**if I open up the clock**—the 42 percent figure references information from: Kim Parker, Juliana Menasce Horowitz, Ruth Igielnik, J. Baxter Oliphant, and Anna Brown, "America's Complex Relationship with Guns," Pew Research Center, 2017. www.pewresearch.org/social-trends/2017/06/22/americas-complex-relationship-with-guns/.

**hour entry:** *the act of saying "orchid"*—with thanks to poet Louise Mathias.

**hour entry:** *The hawk is an approximate whisking together*—information on intervals of a second: Adam Hart-Davis, *The Book of Time: The Secrets of Time, How it Works and How We Measure It* (Buffalo, New York: Firefly Books Ltd., 2011), 32-33.

**20 s. elegy**—written after reading multiple widely reported news stories in 2008 of a private plane hitting a coastal vacation house in Gearhart, Oregon, killing five people, and the news that those in the house had 20 seconds to react. Each line was originally written in the space of 20 seconds. One such source: Michael Rollins, "Five die in plane crash on Oregon Coast," *The Oregonian* (Portland, Oregon), August 4, 2008.

**hour entry:** *I felt I had not done justice*—epigraph quoted from: William James, "The Perception of Time," in *The Principles of Psychology, Volume 1*, (New York: Henry Holt and Company, 1918; Project Gutenberg, 2018), Chapter XV, 605. www.gutenberg.org/files/57628/57628-h/57628-h.htm.

**Other works that informed this project:**

Adrian Bardon, *A Brief History of the Philosophy of Time* (New York: Oxford University Press, 2013).

Barry Dainton, "Temporal Consciousness," *The Stanford Encyclopedia of Philosophy* (Winter 2018 Edition), Edward N. Zalta (ed.), plato.stanford.edu/archives/win2018/entries/consciousness-temporal.

Heraclitus, *Fragments of Heraclitus*, Chapter III, Early Greek Philosophy, English translation by John Burnet (London: A. & C. Black, 1920).

David S. Landes, *Revolution in Time: Clocks and the Making of the Modern World* (Cambridge, Massachusetts, and London: The Belknap Press of Harvard University Press, 1983).

Parmenides, *On Nature, Chapter IV*, Early Greek Philosophy, English translation by John Burnet (London: A. & C. Black, 1920).

Author photo by Emerald Walker

Endi Bogue Hartigan is author of *Pool [5 choruses]* (Omnidawn Publishing, 2014), selected for the Omnidawn Open Book Prize; *One Sun Storm* (Center for Literary Publishing, 2008), selected for the Colorado Prize for Poetry; the chapbook *the seaweed sd treble clef* (Oxeye Press, 2021); and the collaborative chapbook *out of the flowering ribs* (Linda Hutchins and Endi Bogue Hartigan, 2012). Her work has appeared in numerous journals including *West Branch*, *Interim*, *New American Writing*, *VOLT* and others, as well as in collaborative work with artists and writers in the Pacific Northwest.

oh orchid o'clock
by Endi Bogue Hartigan
Cover art by Thérèse Murdza
Interior typefaces: Adobe Jenson Pro and Cronos Pro

Cover and interior design by Endi Bogue Hartigan and Laura Joakimson


Printed in the United States
by Books International, Dulles, Virginia


Publication of this book was made possible in part by gifts from
Katherine & John Gravendyk in honor of Hillary Gravendyk,
Francesca Bell, Mary Mackey, and The New Place Fund


Omnidawn Publishing
Oakland, California
Staff and Volunteers, Spring 2023
Rusty Morrison, senior editor & publisher
Laura Joakimson, executive director
Rob Hendricks, poetry & fiction, & post-pub marketing
Sharon Zetter, poetry editor & book designer
Jeffrey Kingman, copy editor
Liza Flum, poetry editor
Anthony Cody, poetry editor
Jason Bayani, poetry editor
Gail Aronson, fiction editor
Jennifer Metsker, marketing assistant
Sophia Carr, marketing assistant